FIT DECISIONS

CHOOSING A LIFESTYLE OF FITNESS AND FAITH

BY
SONNET FORD-GRANT

Copyright © 2021 by Sonnet Ford-Grant
All rights reserved. No part of this publication may be reproduced distributed, or transmitted in any form or by any means, electronic or mechanical, including photocopying, recording, or by any information storage and retrieval system, without permission in writing from the publisher.
For permission requests, solicit the publisher via the email below.

Absolute Author Publishing House
1123 Williams Blvd., Kenner, LA. 70062
www.absoluteauthor.com

Unless otherwise noted, all Scripture quotations are taken from THE HOLY BIBLE, NEW INTERNATIONAL VERSION ®, NIV® Copyright© 1973, 1978, 1984, 2011 by Biblica, Inc.® Used by permission. All rights reserved worldwide.

Scripture taken from the Holy Bible, The Message, Copyright © 1993, 1994, 1995, 1996, 2000, 2001, 2002 by Eugene H. Peterson.

Scripture taken from the Holy Bible, New Living Translation (NLT), Copyright © 1996, 2004, 2015 by Tyndale House Foundation. Used by permission of Tyndale House Publishers Inc., Carol Stream, Illinois 60199. All rights reserved.

Scripture taken from the New King James Version. Copyright © 1982 by Thomas Nelson, Inc. Used by permission. All rights reserved.
Printed in the United States of America

ISBN: 978-1-64953-340-1

FIT DECISIONS

BY
SONNET FORD-GRANT

ACKNOWLEDGMENTS

Thank you to my husband Fabius, mother Dr. Barbara LeFranc, children Shadre', Katherine, Darius and She'ona, my grandchildren Tramon, Sky and King, and baby brother Ellis. Your support has been a blessing.

Special thanks to Tara Mayers of Journey to Mindful Eating, Darrell Toney of B.U.I.L.T Fitness, Corey Parks of Level 5 Health & Sports Fitness and the L5 family, as well as Barbara Galloway of VI:33, LLC - you have greatly contributed to my fitness journey.

TABLE OF CONTENTS

- **Foreword** 1
- **Introduction** 3
- **Chapter 1:** What Is Fit? 9
- **Chapter 2:** You Gotta Get Moving 15
- **Chapter 3:** What Are You Eating? 39
- **Chapter 4:** Fortify Your Gates 59
- **Chapter 5:** Water, Water, Water! 63
- **Chapter 6:** Stick to It 69
- **Chapter 7:** The Kingdom Perspective 73
- **Accountability Agreement** 79
- **Notes** 83
- **Endnotes** 85

FOREWORD

Very rarely have I picked up a book or piece of literature and read it in its entirety at one sitting. It's usually a few pages per day but this must-read book left me desiring to learn more page after page. It provides the honest approach that making wise choices for a healthier you isn't easy but without a doubt, it is physically and spiritually beneficial. Throughout the book, Dr. Sonnet Ford- Grant shares her own experiences that led to her decision to take control of her life.

As a nurse, I preach a lot of health-related information to my patients, which I sometimes find difficult to practice myself. However, this book gave me much-needed advice and helpful hints to keep me motivated on my fitness journey. As I get older, my desire is to increase strength and energy, as well as practice and maintain healthy choices daily. Dr. Sonnet Ford-Grant has inspired me to achieve these goals.

In this book, she gives sound and practical advice about our overall health. She demonstrates the quality of our health is determined by our choices and fitness goals are not only attainable but a priority for a healthier well-being. Also, she clearly points out we owe it to ourselves to be and stay fit and this only requires a decision. This book definitely will motivate you to get started on your fitness path.

Senaca Lambert

RN BSN CCRN

INTRODUCTION

It all started in June 2019 when my cousin and I took my youngest daughter on a trip to Barbados as a high school graduation gift. While there, we had lunch with a friend who practices mindful eating. She talked to us about food energy, correct portion sizes, ideal mealtimes, and the benefits of healthy eating. Now, while it all sounded good, we spent the rest of the vacation eating whatever and whenever we wanted. It was a vacation, right? Who doesn't go a little overboard while on vacation? I'll wait.

When we returned home to the U.S., vacation fever had lifted. My cousin and I were convicted as we reflected on our friend's words and how we ignored them so easily, giving in to our out-of-control appetites. We also realized our eating habits had outlasted our vacation. Truth be told, they were present before the

Introduction

vacation even began. Unhealthy eating was really our way of life; it just took the vacation and the weight (excuse the pun) of our friend's advice to help us realize it. We knew we needed to make a change. So, we made a deal starting in August (immediately wasn't on the radar), we would clean up our acts and begin making better choices regarding our diets. August came and although it was much easier said than done, we began to put our plan into action with both of us trying to keep our end of the bargain. Neither wanted to be the first to break.

September 13, 2019, my 49th birthday was right around the corner and the realization of how close I was to fifty years old, started weighing on me. Plus, a recent visit to the doctor had revealed that although a small-framed woman, my belly size was out of control. I was approaching the danger zone for developing certain diseases. Having heard this news, I thought about my ancestors' habits and how their health started to decline around my age. Diabetes, high blood pressure and the like were regular visitors to my family. I didn't want them to start hanging out with me. So, at that moment, it became bigger than just a deal. It became a decision. I took control of my life and destiny by deciding from that moment, I would make my health a priority. I would do my part to keep it in good condition. My first step was to change how I ate, but then, the same cousin introduced me to a personal trainer. He invited me to his gym and after one workout I was hooked! The gym became my new happy place, and there was no turning back. Now, it is all about the fit life for me, and I'm loving it!

Not only did my body and mind connect, but my spirit did too. God has taught me many spiritual lessons through this fitness journey. I will share some of them in this book as examples of how fitness and faith are closely connected. I will also help you make the choices that will support your total (mind, body, and spirit) well-being. If someone had told me that one day, I'd be fitness-minded, I would've told them they were crazy. Prior to this transformation, I was neither athletic nor remotely health conscious. But here I am today, a fitness trainer and in the best shape of my life. It is all the result of a decision.

Introduction

Lately, I have met so many people who know they need to do something different when it comes to their health, but who are not ready to make the sacrifice. If you are not dealing with any health issues currently, don't take it for granted. Do not continue practicing bad eating habits and avoiding exercise. Unfortunately, most people wait until something goes wrong to make changes. "Prevention is better than cure" (Desiderius Erasmus). Be preventative. Stop it before it starts. Because make no mistake; it *will* start if the unhealthy patterns continue. If you are already dealing with health issues, it's not too late to turn things around. Significant improvements can be made with a healthy diet, regular exercise, and taking nutritional supplements.

With all the pollution, radiation, toxins, new viruses, and diseases that exist today, being health conscious is more vital than ever. So, I wrote this book to encourage you to take charge of your life by making the solid decision to get fit and live healthy. Giving up your current way of life may seem like a daunting task initially, but once you begin experiencing the benefits, you will see they far outweigh the sacrifices. Your body has served at your pleasure for however long you've been alive. Now, you owe it the opportunity to be and stay fit. As I always say, "healthy is the new sexy." Make the choices necessary to be healthy, starting today!

CHAPTER 1

WHAT IS FIT?

The word "fit" can be used in many ways, but for the sake of this book, it mostly refers to being healthy and in good physical condition. However, being *spiritually* and *mentally* fit will be highlighted as well. Many people have some spiritual base but have neglected to take care of themselves physically. In contrast, others are in great physical and mental shape but don't put much emphasis on spirituality. But the key to overall good health is being physically, mentally, and spiritually fit.

Physical fitness is often viewed from a one-sided perspective: weight, size, and athletic ability. Indeed, these aspects are included, but it is so much more than that. Being fit means engaging in activities that keep the body in shape and operating at its maximum capacity. If neglected, your body can, no let me be frank, *will weaken* (many times prematurely) and succumb to sickness and disease. Being fit entails developing healthy habits to avoid that outcome, and requires solid decision-making, discipline, and determination.

Fitness promotes our overall well-being. It builds confidence, relieves stress, increases energy, fights disease, develops inner and outer strength, and let me not leave out that it keeps us looking good too. Studies show the signs of aging can be prevented or significantly reduced by a fit lifestyle (major plus). Trust me; I don't have a problem with getting old but looking old is not on my wish list.

The Bible encourages us to be physically fit. In 1 Corinthians 6:19, it tells us to take care of our bodies because they are God's temples and He lives within us. We are made up of three parts: spirit, soul and body. Our bodies are one-third of who we are. That's a pretty big deal! Our bodies carry out the desires of our souls and spirits. More importantly, they carry out

Fit Decisions

God's plan and purpose for our lives. When you look at it that way, do you want God living in a raggedy, broken down, and sick temple? No! I answered for you, hope you don't mind. You want it to be in tip-top shape, so you can accomplish the assignments you were put here to do.

I recently watched a movie I had seen several times, but this time as I watched, it hit differently. If you've read my first book, *What Should I Do? A Practical Guide for* Good Decision-*Making,*[1] *av*ailable on Amazon, I guess you've noticed I'm a movie kind of girl. It was the movie *World War Z*[2], starring Brad Pitt. It was about a zombie pandemic that had spread throughout the world. The zombies would go after people and infect them. Then, the infected people would turn into zombies and the cycle would continue. But something significant was discovered during the pandemic. The zombies would never go after anyone who was sick. It was later revealed why. The zombies avoided sick people because they knew they could not fully thrive within a sick host. Now, please don't get all twisted up in a knot. I am by no means comparing God to a zombie but what was revealed to me is God cannot thrive and fully operate as He wants to through a sick body. Sure, He can use anybody, but His desire is for us to be healthy and strong, so that through us, His strength and goodness can be revealed (more on this in Chapter 7). I do understand because we live in an imperfect world, sometimes things just come upon us. But it is our responsibility to protect our bodies from harm. Taking care of our bodies shows we value and are thankful for them.

"After all, no one ever hated their own body, but they feed and care for their body, just as Christ does the church" (Ephesians 5:29).

This is a beautiful picture and a great example. If you know anything about how Christ feels about the church, you know that He loves it, protects it, takes care of it and thanked His heavenly Father for giving it to Him. When it comes to our bodies, we should follow suit. We are not supposed to idolize flesh, but we certainly can't minimize its importance. During the 17 years I pastored a church and as a Doctor of Divinity, I was focused on encouraging people to be fit spiritually, without also sharing the importance of being fit physically (my bad). Although strengthening our spirits is the most important thing, scripture encourages us to be fit in our bodies.

"Exercise daily in God—no spiritual flabbiness, please! Workouts in the gymnasium are useful, but a disciplined life in God is far more so, making you fit both today and forever" (1 Timothy 4:8, The Message).

Now that you have a better understanding of what fit is, its importance and benefits, are you ready to move forward? If so, I'm so excited for you! Yay! You are on your way to healthy living.

CHAPTER 2

YOU GOTTA GET MOVING

Movement is life and is a major part of fitness. The body should be physically active or exercising on a regular basis. However, make sure before starting any exercise regimen you consult your physician. Statistics show 28 percent of Americans aged six and older are physically inactive.[3] Twenty-eight percent may not sound like a lot, but it's more than eighty million people. That's huge!

Now, while I'm spitting out these statistics and shedding light on the lack of physical activity, I am by no means judging. I was once a part of this fit-less (if that's even a word) crew. In fact, I would often joke by telling people who were trying to get me on the fitness trail I was allergic to exercise. I just had a hard time getting with the program. I remember a time my husband and I traveled to Pennsylvania to visit his family. My sister-in-love, who is an avid exerciser, invited me to go to the gym with her. To be polite, I accepted the invitation but although I made it through the workout (barely), I had no desire to return. So, trust me; I get it. But now I know better and when you know better what happens? You do better. I want to help as many people as I can do better. Does that mean because I am a fitness trainer, I have all the answers? Am I an expert on *all things* related to health and wellness? No. In fact, when God put it in my spirit to share this message, I reminded him of that reality. His answer to me was, "you don't need to know it all, just be a voice and a role model." *Sir, yes Sir!* However, from the knowledge and experience I do have, I can tell you that getting in fit mode is a wise choice because it truly makes a difference.

"Exercise is activity requiring physical effort carried out to sustain or improve health and fitness."[4] It falls into four main categories: strength, endurance, balance and flexibility. My favorite is strength but incorporating all four into your exercise regimen offers the greatest benefit. I will take time to briefly discuss each category and the life lessons that can be learned within each one.

STRENGTH

Another name for "strength training" is "resistance training." Strength exercises build muscle and help us perform everyday activities like lifting boxes, carrying groceries, and climbing stairs, to name a few. Strength training exercises include:

- Using our own bodyweight
- Lifting weights (using dumbbells or free weights)
- Using resistance bands

Using bodyweight to build muscle can be effective, but it takes a little longer than using weights.

Some of the benefits of strength training are:

- Stronger bones and joints to reduce the risk of injury
- Retention of muscle mass
- Weight loss by controlling body fat
- Improved physical appearance

I must point out here no matter what, some decrease in muscle mass occurs with aging (sarcopenia); however, strength training can keep this at a minimum. Physically inactive people lose about three to five percent muscle mass per decade after the age of thirty. For best results, strength training should take place at least two to three times a week with rest days in between. Muscles need 24 to 48 hours to recover, repair and rebuild. It is a good idea to have a coach or trainer, as they are experienced and will know how to guide you in the right direction (hint, hint). However, many people work out on their own. If you go the latter route, make sure you know what you're doing; otherwise, lack of desired results and serious injury can occur.

When it comes to strength training, there are some great lessons to be learned. I would never have thought building natural muscles could teach so much about building spiritual muscles. With strength training, there is something called "progressive overload." It means with time the weights or resistance must get heavier and more difficult if the muscles are to grow bigger. When the weight is increased, it challenges the muscles to go beyond their comfort zone, push harder and grow bigger to handle the pressure that is coming against them. The result is called, "muscle gains." *Yeah baby!*

In life, we don't like it when things press or come against us, but that's how strength is developed. Sometimes God allows challenges because He wants more growth to take place in our lives. He knows if the weight is too light, we won't grow to our full potential. He wants us to be good at strength training. So, every now and then, when things get heavy, He is implementing progressive overload into our lives resulting in bigger muscles. Use the following scripture as inspiration for both your natural and spiritual strength training workouts.

"But the more they afflicted them, the more they multiplied and grew" (Exodus 1:12, New King James Version).

ENDURANCE

Pump it up, pump it up, pump it up! Ok, let me calm down, but endurance training is all about getting our blood pumping and heart thumping. Our breathing and heart rates increase with these types of exercises. It is known as "cardio" because it incorporates movements that strengthen the heart. It also helps keep the lungs and circulatory system healthy. Cardio exercises include, but are not limited to the following:

- Walking (briskly)
- Jogging
- Running
- Bike riding
- Swimming
- Dancing (*my personal favorite*)

Anything of an aerobic (requiring free oxygen) nature is considered cardio. Doing one or more of these exercises daily for at least twenty to thirty minutes can help prevent, improve, or eliminate conditions such as, type 2 diabetes, heart disease, high blood pressure, obesity, some forms of cancer and other ailments.

About a year before I made the decision to get fit, my doctor gave me the Boston Heart Fatty Acid Balance™ test, which measures the major fatty acids to help identify cardiovascular disease. My test results showed plaque was building up in my arteries. My doctor explained that arteries carry blood away from the heart, while veins carry blood to the heart. Any blockages to that process would compromise my entire circulatory system and put my heart in danger. She suggested a diet change and daily exercise. I must admit, even that diagnosis wasn't enough to prompt me into action, but it was always in the back of my mind. Now that I have changed my diet and exercise regularly, I am proud to say that according to a more recent test, the plaque has decreased significantly, and my arteries are looking good. As the saying goes, "You can't beat a healthy heart." When our hearts are not healthy, it leads to all types of unpleasant physical issues. And just so you know, it works the same way in a spiritual sense.

"Above all else, guard your heart, for everything you do flows from it" (Proverbs 4:23).

Cardio exercises work extremely well for weight loss. Past the 20-minute mark usually puts us in the fat-burning zone, where our bodies begin to use stored fat for energy. Although cardio exercises help with this process, it is important to couple them with strength training, as this will help us maintain muscle mass while losing weight.

So, what are you waiting for? Get to stepping (literally)! Your health depends on it. Your neighborhood, home, the gym, parks, and recreation centers are all great places to get it done. You can check out YouTube where there are tons of channels that provide great aerobic workouts. However, hiring a personal trainer enforces accountability. On your own, you won't always be motivated to put in the work. A certified personal trainer is qualified to create a program to suit your personal needs.

BALANCE

Beyond exercise, balance is something that should be practiced in every area of our lives. It keeps things in order and stable. Too often in life, we stay too close to the shore or go too far out in the ocean, never finding the perfect balance (Work with me here, I figured beach talk would paint a clearer picture). In other words, balance is necessary to live a healthy and happy life.

In terms of fitness, balance is vital. Without it, any activity would be too hard to do. Fortunately, there are exercises that can help to improve it. Pretty much any movement that challenges our center of gravity is considered a balance exercise. As we age, the risk of falling becomes greater due to decreased physical strength and bone density. And while the younger generation may think they're exempt, this decrease begins between the ages of 25 and 30. So, we all should be working to strengthen our balance game. If needed, Google "balance exercises" to see examples and to get a more thorough list of activities you can do.

FLEXIBILITY

A little flexibility goes a long way. When we're too rigid, it can stifle, or should I say, stiffen movement. To get the most out of life, we must be willing to be stretched beyond our normal levels of comfort. I'm talking about more than exercise right now, so please be flexible (chuckle) in your thinking. I throw in little wisdom nuggets where I can.

Ok, so let's move on to the topic at hand. Flexibility exercises consist of stretching. During these movements, the muscles are stretched to enable more, (you guessed it; you're so smart) flexibility. Stretching exercises don't necessarily help with strength or endurance, but they do allow you to move more freely when performing other exercises or your daily activities. Stretching is also good after sitting or riding for a long period of time. This helps to loosen tight muscles. According to the American Heart Association (heart.org), stretching exercises should be done when muscles are already warm to allow them to stretch farther without discomfort or pain.5 To warm your muscles try walking in place for three to five minutes.

INTENTIONAL MOVEMENT

In the movie "Karate Kid" (starring Jaden Smith and Jackie Chan), Mr. Haan told Dre', while he was training him, "Everything is karate."[6] He just had to realize it. Well as you're reading this, I represent Mr. Haan and I'm telling you everything can be exercise. You just have to realize it and decide to do it. Let me show you what I'm talking about.

- The next time you are cooking in the kitchen and stirring that pot, don't just stir to be stirring; focus on your arm and shoulder, then move them around in a circular motion engaging the muscles. Do this for at least one minute and then switch to the other arm. Exercise each arm at least three times for the one-minute duration.
- While your food is cooking, this is a great time to get in some steps by walking around briskly.

- When getting out of bed, use that motion to do some sit-ups. You will have literally accomplished something before even getting up.
- Headed to the mall or grocery store? Park a little further away and then briskly walk to the entrance; take the stairs instead of the elevator; or climb the escalator instead of riding it.
- And how about those groceries? When you return home from shopping, grab one or two of your heaviest bags and do some bicep curls.

Now, you have a few examples. I'm confident you will get creative and connect your mind and body to come up with your own moves while you are going about your day. But don't take the easy way out. Keep in mind this is not to replace regular exercise routines. These are just additional things you can do to keep you in a movement state of mind and to enhance the fitness process.

ADDITIONAL BENEFITS

So far, I have covered some of the benefits of exercise, but I'd like to add a few more. Before I do, let it be known although I will include statistical information, these are benefits I have personally experienced. A few of my family members have reaped some of the benefits as well. As you embrace this lifestyle, you more than likely will experience them too. The benefits I mention are not an exhaustive list, but hopefully, they will inspire you. It is my aim to provide you with enough information to jump-start healthy living.

GET YOUR SLEEP ON

One thing I love is some good sleep. My family often teases me about my frequent meetings with the "Sandman." For those not familiar with that term, it's a personification of that feeling of sand in your eyes when you start getting sleepy. But my sleep pattern had started to change. Not sure why, but I was no longer sleeping through the night. Then along came exercise and the Sandman and I were once again united. My mom had a long bout with insomnia but will now tell you exercising on a regular basis has turned that around. The point is exercise can improve sleep quality dramatically.

Getting at least eight hours of sleep per night is essential for optimum health. However, 30 percent of employed adults report obtaining six hours or less of sleep per night.[7] Moreover, significant sleep complaints are reported by approximately one-third of all adults.[8] It is not known exactly how exercise is connected to better sleep. However, some suggest it is because it helps to reduce stress, stabilize your mood, and decompress the mind, which are all important components of falling asleep naturally.[9] A study of more than 2,600 men and women, ages 18 to 85, found that 150 minutes per week of moderate to vigorous physical activity, provided a 65 percent improvement in sleep quality.[10] When you break it down, that is just thirty minutes per day for five days per week. Not so bad, right? You can do it! If a good night's sleep has been challenging for you, try a little exercise. The Sandman is waiting to greet you.

BOOSTED ENERGY

Feeling sluggish? Need an energy boost? Guess what? Exercise helps with that too! Stop overdosing on coffee and energy drinks and just get moving. When exercising, endorphins (our happy hormones) are released: they give a burst of energy and provide a feeling of euphoria. Aahhh! And since exercise helps you sleep better at night *and* boosts cardiovascular health, it allows you to have more energy and endurance throughout the day. I like the sound of that, don't you?

THE B.M. EFFECT

It may be a little gross to talk about, but I couldn't leave this one out. When I tell you exercise can get you going, believe it. "Going where?" you ask. It can get you going to the bathroom and going quite regularly. I will just go on and put my business out there by telling you my dirty little secret. All ears, aren't you? Until I got into the fitness groove, I frequently dealt with constipation. Turns out, I was not alone. According to the National Institute of

Diabetes and Digestive and Kidney Diseases, constipation is one of the most common gastrointestinal problems in the United States and about 42 million Americans persistently suffer from it. "Lack of physical activity can contribute to constipation."[11]

Regular exercise can lead to more frequent bowel movements by promoting activity in the digestive tract. In other words, when you get moving, your bowels can too. And oh, what a relief it is! The bloated feeling goes away and you feel much lighter. Bowel movements are nature's way of ridding the body of solid waste. Although there is no set standard for how many bowel movements you should have per day, going at least once daily is a pretty good goal. However, if you are going longer than three days without a release, that could indicate a problem. At that point, you should act. Talk to your doctor; get some fiber in your system or move your body. Even if you choose to do the first two, throwing in the last one is not a bad idea.

DEPRESSION RELIEF

Yep, might as well be honest and admit I've dealt with depression too. After all, you can't help somebody with what you haven't been through yourself. I have never been to the point where I've needed medication, but I have experienced many dark days, been overwhelmed by my thoughts, and paralyzed by the pain of my circumstances. That's right me, the Minister, but I'm human and life happens to us all. Sure, I read the following scriptures:

> "Cast all your anxiety on him because he cares for you" (1 Peter 5:7).
> "The weapons we fight with are not the weapons of the world. On the contrary, they have divine power to demolish strongholds" (2 Corinthians 10:4).
> "I can do all this through him who gives me strength" (Philippians 4:13).

And believe me; these verses kept me holding on through the process and moving forward during the pain. But through fitness, God helped me find a practical way to live out those scriptures. When I'm lifting that weighted ball and then slamming it to the ground, I see myself casting off my cares and giving them to God. At the same time, I fight back by casting down all thoughts that serve me no purpose. When I pick up those dumbbells, I recognize and harness the strength of Christ and know He's working through me. Through exercise, I present my body as a living sacrifice (Romans 12:1) and call those things that do not yet exist as though they already do (Romans 4:17). As a result, my body reacts and responds. When I get moving, I feel in my soul I am more than a conqueror (Romans 8:31) and all things are possible (Mark 9:23). Through fitness, I am learning how to be disciplined physically, mentally, and spiritually.

"I discipline my body like an athlete, training it to do what it should" (1 Corinthians 9:27, New Living Translation).

Whew! Now I got that all out, let me say depression is a monster that steals joy and crushes hope, but exercise is a way of escape.

God promises to provide that for us whenever temptation shows up.

"No temptation has overtaken you except what is common to mankind. And God is faithful; he will not let you be tempted beyond what you can bear. But when you are tempted, he will also provide a way out so that you can endure it" (1Corinthians 10:13).

Once you start working out, your mind gets a break from your problems; clarity comes, and you focus on ways to improve yourself. In turn, this brings answers and solutions to your problems. When depression shows up at your door, slam that door in its face and take your way of escape. I'm not saying exercise is the only way, but it is one way that works. Don't just take my word for it. Studies show exercise is an all-natural treatment for depression and in some cases, as effective as drugs.[12] That said, please take your medicine if necessary and follow your doctor's orders.

If you've been battling depression, my prayer is hope finds its way to you. Life is meant to be lived and enjoyed. God wants you healthy, happy, and whole. There's light at the end of the tunnel. May you find that light through God's Word, exercise, and healthy living.

FEELING HOT, HOT, HOT!

I hope you're ready because this thing is about to get juicy! It's a benefit truly worth sharing. Due to the sensitivity of the subject, I was going to leave it out, but I got the green light from Heaven to tell it like it is. This fit life has increased my libido (sex drive). Not that there was a problem before, but it has gone to a whole new level, which has made my husband an even happier man. Maybe it's the confidence that working out brings. Maybe it's the release of all those endorphins, or perhaps it's the increased energy. Whatever it is, it is working honey!

Dr. Tina M. Penhollow, an associate professor in the Department of Exercise Science and Health Promotion at Florida Atlantic University says, "Being active is a potent aphrodisiac for both men and women" (I sense somebody putting their gym clothes on right now). According to Dr. Penhollow, aerobic exercise increases blood flow and improves circulation, which are key factors to sexual response. She goes on to discuss how strength training increases libido as well. A study by the University of California found that, for men, regular exercise significantly enhanced "frequency of various intimate activities, the reliability of adequate functioning during sex, [and] percentage of satisfying orgasms." Research done by the University of Texas revealed exercise increases "physiological sexual arousal in women."[13] In layman's terms, that means, after a workout, these ladies are more likely to be sexually aroused than those who haven't exercised.

Well, if nothing else made you want to get fit, that should motivate you. Sex is a beautiful thing. It is to be enjoyed between two people to express their love for one another. God created and approved it (see scripture below). If your marriage could use some spicing up in the bedroom, regular exercise could be just the thing that rekindles the fire and turns up the heat. Try it out and see what happens.

"The wife gives authority over her body to her husband, and the husband gives authority over his body to his wife. Do not deprive each other of sexual relations unless you both agree to refrain from sexual intimacy for a limited time so you can give yourselves more completely to prayer. Afterward, you should come together again so that Satan won't be able to tempt you because of your lack of self-control" (1 Corinthians 7:4-5, New Living Translation).

CHANGE FROM THE INSIDE OUT

It can be extremely frustrating when you're putting effort into something but feel as if you're not getting any results. This is the case initially with many of my fitness clients. They start with a vision in mind but, if that vision doesn't show up quickly enough, they feel as if nothing is happening. That couldn't be further from the truth. I explain to them even though the outward changes haven't shown up yet, wonderful changes are taking place on the inside. The proof is in their doctors' reports.

Prior to exercising regularly, their test numbers were out of whack, but now, their insides have come alive. They breathe better and have lowered their blood pressure and A1C levels (blood sugar). Their cells are responding favorably and joints that were once locked up, have loosened up. Soon, the outer changes they longed for start to show up.

Faith works the same way. As you embrace it, things start happening within you that can't be seen with physical eyes but are producing positive energy. Eventually, as you continue to put your faith into practice, that positive energy begins to shine through. It manifests physical results that are obvious to you and others. In either situation, as you continue to move forward, even though you may not see it yet, change is happening from the inside out.

CHAPTER 3

WHAT ARE YOU EATING?

The other part of being and staying fit is diet. To be honest, it's probably the most important part. Afterall, you can't out-exercise a bad diet. You can do all the physical movements in the world, but if your diet is poor, you won't get the optimum results. The Western or Standard American Diet (S.A.D.) is how can I put it? Sad! Its acronym says it all. It is loaded with sugars, highly processed foods, butter, fried foods, unhealthy fats, and the like. This type of diet is mouthwatering and delicious but can lead to obesity. And don't be fooled, obesity is not necessarily the person who measures on the higher end of the scale. A person can be small-framed, measuring on the lower end of the scale and still be obese. It has to do with body composition.

I am five feet tall (no short jokes, please), and before my fitness journey, I weighed 135 pounds. I was consuming too much of the wrong kinds of food. To others, I looked small, but my body fat percentage was in the obese range. Who knew? And like many people, my mid-section is the area where I gain the most fat. Both my waist size and my body fat percentage indicated I was in the health risk range. The belly is the hotbed for the onset of disease. When too much visceral (deep belly) fat accumulates, it begins to surround the vital organs. Let's just say this can cause some major damage. I suggest you find out your waist size and body fat percentage as they will help you determine if you are in the healthy range. There are different ways this can be done. Although you can do it yourself, I recommend seeing your doctor or a personal trainer.

Healthy body fat percentages vary depending on who you ask. Refer to the chart below as a suggested guide.

Age Range	Men Healthy %	Women Healthy %
20-39 yrs.	8-19%	21-33%
40-59 yrs.	11-22%	23-35%
60-79 yrs.	13-25%	24-36%

Healthy Percentage Body Fat Chart from: Common Sense Health.com

"Body Fat Chart for Healthy Body Fat Percentage" *Commonsensehealth.com*

According to the American Heart Association, optimal waist sizes are below 35 inches for women and below 40 inches for men.[14]

EAT GOOD, FEEL GOOD

If you're going to live fit, you must eat healthy. It requires some adjustments but is so worth it in the end. Since I've been enlightened, some of the foods I didn't like before are now a regular part of my meals. For instance, around age seven, I tasted avocado for the first time. It was an instant no-no. I couldn't stand the taste. I immediately spit it out. It took me forty-two years to even think about trying it again. Today, give me an avocado with some sweet red peppers, sprinkled with a little garlic salt and black pepper, and I'm good! I eat it at least twice per week. Tastebuds tend to conform when you show them who's boss and let them know they have no other choice.

When you eat good, you feel good. Your system is clean and satisfied. You can feel the energy flowing through you. A poor diet may taste good but will keep you feeling sluggish and fatigued. I remember growing up hearing my father say, "What's good to you ain't always good for you and what's good for you ain't always good to you." He was right, but when wisdom kicks in, you get creative and find ways to make what's good for you, good to you. The positive results become the bigger picture.

GOOD FUEL

Some people highlight one diet over others. They make a big deal about either being vegetarian, pescatarian, or an all-things-meat lover. Each diet has its benefits, but as a personal trainer, as well as a person of faith, I'm not judging. And looking at the following scriptures, it's apparent God isn't tripping over it either:

> "Everything that lives and moves about will be food for you. Just as I gave you the green plants, I now give you everything" (Genesis 9:3).
>
> "Do not destroy the work of God for the sake of food. All food is clean, but it is wrong for a person to eat anything that causes someone to stumble" (Romans 14:20).
>
> "I know and am convinced on the authority of the Lord Jesus that no food, in and of itself, is wrong to eat. But if someone believes it is wrong, then for that person it is wrong" (Romans 14:14, New Living Translation).
>
> "For instance, one person believes it's all right to eat anything. But another believer with a sensitive conscience will eat only vegetables" (Romans 14:2, New Living Translation).

It's all good (literally). I just hope you eat healthily and sensibly no matter what style of eating you choose. Bottom line is our bodies need food for fuel to keep us going from day to day. But as it is with a car, if you put cheap gas in it, its performance will show it. And I am a firm believer, you are what you eat. Therefore, if you want your body to run well, you must provide it with good fuel.

FRUITS AND VEGETABLES

Fruits and vegetables (raw and organic are best) should be a major part of your everyday eating, as they provide a variety of nutrients with fewer calories. Health professionals recommend you to "eat the rainbow." What that means is, to include a colorful array of fruits and vegetables in your diet. Their colors reveal some of the benefits they provide:

- Orange foods for example, help protect against cancer and have beta-carotene which the body converts into vitamin A. Our bodies need vitamin A for good vision, healthy skin, and strong immune systems.

- Reds are good for fighting free radicals. Free radicals are unstable molecules that can cause damage to cells within the body.
- Yellows provide nutrients that help the cells in the body to communicate.
- Greens help protect the immune system, fight off bacteria and viruses and offer lots of calcium.
- Purple and blue hues provide folic acid, fiber, and iron. They are powerful antioxidants in the body. "They're known for maintaining a healthy heart and memory function," says, San Francisco-based dietitian, Corrine Dobbas, MS, RD.
- White fruits and vegetables have immune boosting properties and can help lower bad cholesterol levels, as well as blood pressure levels.[15]

Essentially, the more colors you eat, the more nutrients you are taking in and the more benefits you'll receive.

PROTEIN

You should also include protein in your daily diet. It is important for every cell in the body. Our hair and nails are made up of mostly protein. Protein helps with building strong muscles, repairing tissues, making enzymes, hormones, and other bodily chemicals. Some good sources of protein are:

- Fish
- Shrimp
- Eggs
- Milk
- Greek yogurt
- Nuts (almonds & peanuts)
- Lean beef
- Chicken breast

Of course, you should find out if you are allergic to any of these foods before consuming them. Your doctor may be able to perform an allergen test that can expose foods that do not agree with you. Eating food you are allergic to can cause bad reactions: itching, skin rashes, and breathing problems. Allergic reactions can also lead to illness or even death.

CARBOHYDRATES

Next on the list are carbohydrates (carbs). They are important to a healthy diet. These are the body's main source of energy. The digestive system converts them into glucose or blood sugar which gets used as energy for the cells, tissues, and organs. Now, there are good carbs and bad carbs. Which ones do you want to hear first? I'll start with the good, some of which have already been mentioned like fruits, vegetables, and milk products (which also contain protein and fat). Some others are:

- Kidney beans (high in protein)
- Oats
- Quinoa
- Sweet potatoes
- Chickpeas
- Beets

And here comes the bad:

- White pasta
- White rice
- White bread
- Sweets and pastries made with white flour
- Sodas
- Beer

Consuming these carbs in excess can cause your health to go south. Avoid the temptation to overload on them.

FATS

Although fat is the thing most of us are trying to get rid of, incorporating it makes for a well-balanced diet. Some healthy sources of fat are:

- Avocado
- Extra virgin olive oil
- Pecans
- Chia seeds
- Flax seeds
- Fatty fish

Please note while these foods are good for us, they are still "fats." If consumed too much, we may pack on some unwanted pounds, which is probably not the result most of us are looking for.

IT'S TIME TO PUT THE FORK DOWN!

All-you-can-eat buffet style restaurants draw hundreds of people to their locations daily. They know the all-you-can-eat concept is appealing to just about anyone who is hungry. In these restaurants people pile mile-high food on their plates and go back for more and more. While consuming all the food you can may be a good perk, is it a good decision?

The Japanese have caught onto something that significantly reduces their risk of serious illnesses and causes them to live longer than average (one hundred plus years). It is a principle the Okinawans have lived by for centuries that helps keep their eating under control. The principle is called "hara hachi bu" which means fill your belly to only eighty percent. You do this by eating what is required to no longer be hungry rather than eating until you are stuffed. Pay attention to your portions and start learning to determine what eighty percent of fullness is for you. This will get easier with time and practice.

It is important to note the speed at which you eat can contribute to mindless overeating. Psychologist, Susan Albers, suggests to, "slow down while eating and give your body time to register how much you've eaten. If you eat quickly and stop at what you think is eighty percent full, you may actually be one hundred percent full and not know it since your body hasn't caught up yet with your mind."[16] There's no rush! Slowing down keeps your mind connected to the process and helps you enjoy your food even more.

Overeating doesn't just happen in restaurants. It also happens in homes every day. Boredom, anxiety, depression, and many other things can lead to emotional eating. While we may not like to admit it, sometimes it's just greed. Our eyes get bigger than our stomachs and we overload. So, from now on, when you are tempted to overeat, decide to use the hara hachi bu technique to help you fight. Can you say, "hara hachi bu?"

PROCESSED FOODS

As much as possible, try to limit eating highly processed foods, which are foods that have been significantly altered during preparation. These foods have gone through many mechanical and chemical processes mainly for taste enhancement and/or preservation. They contain large amounts of sugars, sodium and fat, and usually have high-calorie counts, but lack nutritional value. Also, because the taste has been dramatically enhanced, we tend to go overboard when eating them. This piles on calories that provide temporary pleasure but in the long run, will do us no good. Here is a list, to give you an idea of what I'm talking about:

- Hotdogs (I know. I love them too.)
- Bacon (oh no!)
- Boxed or packaged noodles (sorry kids and college crew.)

- Baked goods like pastries and cakes (this is a tough one for me.)
- Canned soups (appear healthy, but most have too much sodium.)
- Cereals (are usually high in sugar.)
- Bread (is often chemically loaded.)
- Potato chips (you know you can't eat just one.)
- Fried foods (causes oil overload.)

Trust me, I don't mean to be a killjoy. I understand the things on this list are comfort foods and very delicious. I'm crazy about some of them too. But I have come to realize how they are wreaking havoc on our bodies silently; therefore, my assignment is to sound the alarm.

Now, let me say this, even when you buy food in its natural state, as you cook it and add ingredients, the food is being processed. But how you cook it and what you add to it is what makes the difference. So not all processed food is bad. Just be smart about your ingredients and preparation methods.

LEARN A NEW HOBBY

A hobby is usually something to be enjoyed, but like it or not, please start this one. Before buying *anything*, read the label (both the nutrition facts and ingredients). Make it a habit. Be like Santa Claus and check the list twice, so you can find out what's naughty and what's nice. That may sound corny, but you get the picture.

My husband and children tease me because I have become the label-reading queen. We must look out for ourselves because many ingredients being added to foods by the manufacturers that are approved by the FDA for human consumption, have harmful long-term effects. I will not spend much time on this but beware of dyes, chemicals, allergens, sweeteners, and anything that could be potentially harmful.

ADDED SUGAR IS THE DEVIL

The subtitle may be a little too dramatic, but I want to make sure I have your attention. Added sugar is not our friend. Take it from me. I was once a sugar addict. I couldn't get enough of it until I discovered all its negative effects. Now, a little sugar here and there is cool. It occurs naturally in some foods such as fruit (fructose) and milk (lactose). But when all the other sugary stuff gets added (sucrose or table sugar) and eaten in excess that can cause health issues. Sodas, fruit juices, candy, doughnuts, and items I've previously listed are included in the added sugars category. Too much sugar (even the natural kind) can lead to:

- Acne
- Obesity
- Inflammation
- Heart disease
- Stroke
- Diabetes

The American Heart Association recommends no more than 36 grams (nine teaspoons) per day of added sugar for men; and no more than 25 grams (six teaspoons) per day of added sugar for women and children.[17] With that being said, I must warn you that just one 12 ounce can of Coke contains 39 grams (9.75 teaspoons) of added sugar, gasp! We must be

Fit Decisions

careful. The food and drinks we consume daily may appear harmless, but when you look at them closely, you find out the real deal. As I stated before, start a hobby of checking labels. For the most part, manufacturers list the ingredients and nutritional information of the foods and drinks they make. Compare what's listed to the recommended daily consumption so you can make fit decisions.

If you have a sweet tooth that won't leave you alone, there are alternatives. Do your research to find healthy sugar substitutes and then make your choice. Also, dark chocolate is not only tasty, but it is also considered to be healthy. It is made from cacao beans which are rich in antioxidants. Look for dark chocolate that has at least seventy percent cacao. This ensures the fat and sugar contents are low. The darker the chocolate, the more bitter the taste, but it still contains some sugar, so as far as sweet cravings go, it may do the trick.

LET'S TALK CALORIES

There's a lot of talk about calories but some people may not know what they are. Simply put, a calorie is a unit used to measure energy. Each food has a certain amount of energy it releases when consumed. Proteins and carbohydrates contain four calories per gram, while fats contain nine calories per gram. One pound of fat is equal to 3500 calories. So, whether you want to gain or reduce weight, you'll have to add or subtract 3500 calories. For example, since there are seven days in a week, to lose one pound per week, you would have to reduce your diet by five hundred calories per day (7 X 500 = 3500 calories). To gain, you will have to add at least five hundred calories per day to your diet. A good way to get on track for either result is to find out your Basal Metabolic Rate (BMR) and your Total Daily Energy Expenditure (TDEE). Your BMR is a count of the total calories or energy your body needs to perform its basic, life-sustaining functions when at rest, like breathing, pumping blood, digesting food, sleeping, and other involuntary processes.

The TDEE is an estimate of calories burned when you factor in your activity level. I know this sounds like a lot, but there are online calculators that can help you figure it out. Alternatively, you can see a dietician or once again, hire a personal trainer. Once you know how many calories your body needs to perform all its functions, to include your activities, you will then know what adjustments to make, to either maintain your current weight, or to gain or lose weight. Basically, burning the same calories you consume will help you maintain your current weight. Taking in more calories than you burn will cause you to gain weight and burning more calories than you consume will cause you to lose weight.

CHEATING IS ALLOWED

Now don't let your thoughts run away with you. We are only talking about food here. Once you have developed healthier eating habits and are consistent with exercising, one or two days of eating the food you love is okay. My day of indulgence is Saturday. Oh, how I just love

Saturdays! On this day (and sometimes the next day), the food I have been desiring but denying myself all week gets lovingly embraced. I take my time eating them bite by bite and relishing every moment. After that, I get back on track with sensible, healthy eating. What I'm trying to say is, food is meant to be enjoyed. I mean *all* the fun can't be taken away. If you choose the weekends or some other day to go for the gusto (don't go too far though), it's not the end of the world. As soon as possible (like right away), resume your healthy eating habits.

CHAPTER 4

FORTIFY YOUR GATES

In ancient times, some kings would build walls around their city gates for protection. These were called, "fortified cities." To fortify means to strengthen with defensive efforts to protect against attack. The walls were built to keep enemies from entering and causing destruction.

As a child of God, you are a part of His kingdom and considered a king (men and women). It is your responsibility to fortify your gates and protect your city. In other words, protect what has been given to you. In this case, your city is your body. This imperfect world we live in has a plethora of bacteria, viruses and conditions that cause illness and disease. But with a strong gate we can protect ourselves. Let's look at our body's primary gate.

THE IMMUNE SYSTEM

In the above analogy, the gates represent your immune system. It has a very important function. It is your defense system, which is made up of several complex biological structures and processes that protect against infections and diseases. The main components of this system are:

- White blood cells
- Lymph nodes
- Antibodies
- The spleen
- Bone marrow
- The thymus
- The Complement System

When your immune system is weak, it has a hard time fighting off foreign invaders. One of the major things that can weaken your immune system is stress. When you get too stressed out, your body goes from an alkaline state (where disease can't flourish) to an acidic state (Disney World for germs, and disease-causing agents). Therefore, it is important to do what you can to eliminate stress by learning how to rid or manage anything that adds it to your life.

The immune system, which has memory cells, is highly intelligent. It keeps a record of every virus it has ever defeated. If a virus tries to come back, the immune system recognizes it and quickly launches an all-out attack, destroying it before it can multiply and make you sick. Pretty neat trick, don't you think? Some viruses like the flu and common cold must be fought many times because of the different strains that exist.

You can fortify your gates or keep your immune system balanced and strong in many ways. These include:

- Healthy diet
- Exercise
- Vitamins, herbs, and supplements
- Not smoking
- Limiting alcohol consumption
- Good hygiene
- Adequate sleep

Regarding vitamins, I want to highlight the necessity of vitamin D. It is essential to the proper functioning of the immune system. It can help to decrease inflammation and promote an immune response. It is also known to help with protection against respiratory diseases (so needed in this age of COVID-19 and other coronaviruses). To get vitamin D in your system, eat foods like salmon, mushrooms, and egg yolks. And don't be afraid of the sun. Vitamin D is sometimes called, "the sunshine vitamin."[18] When exposed to sunlight, the body naturally produces Vitamin D. You can also get vitamin D through supplements. Talk to your doctor to find out the dosage that's right for you.

Do your due diligence. It's up to you. The things mentioned above can keep infections at bay. Remember, you are the king in the story. When you fortify your gates (your immune system) and protect your city (your body), the enemies (viruses, germs, diseases) may huff and puff, but they won't be able to blow your house (your health) down.

CHAPTER 5

WATER, WATER, WATER!

When I was in my early twenties, I worked at a dialysis center. Day in and day out I saw patients connected to machines that helped to filter their blood because their kidneys no longer functioned. Without this procedure, toxins would build up in their bodies, leading to death. I remember one day as I was doing my rounds, checking patient stats so that I could update charts, an elderly patient said something to me that has always stuck in my mind. He looked at me and with the sincerest tone said, "Young lady, whatever you do, drink water. Lack of water is what has me here." I didn't understand it all then, but as time went on and as I had family members who dealt with kidney problems, I learned the value of drinking water.

Water, Water, Water!

Water helps your kidneys rid waste from your blood through urination. It also helps to keep your blood vessels open so blood can travel without restriction to your kidneys and provide them with essential nutrients. If you become dehydrated, it is difficult for this process to take place. Dehydration occurs when the cells don't have enough water to properly function. Dehydration can lead to all kinds of medical problems:

- Kidney damage
- Asthma
- Arthritis
- Allergies
- Stiffness
- Pain
- Brain fog

Drinking sufficient water each day is an important part of maintaining good health. Our body is made up of about sixty to seventy percent water and every part of our body needs water to do the job it was designed to do. The body can go up to three weeks without food but can only go three or four days without water. This gives some insight into how important water is to life. Health authorities commonly recommend we drink at least half of our body weight in ounces of water each day. Therefore, if you weigh 150 pounds, 75 ounces of water per day should be your goal. Weigh yourself and then do the math. Personally, I try to drink a gallon of water (128 ounces) three days per week (and half my body weight on other days). That's not an easy task, but It flushes out my system and helps keep me hydrated for the busy life I lead. Find what works best for your body and then make sure you're drinking that amount regularly. Oh, and as an incentive to get you drinking enough water, it can help with weight loss too. Is that enough motivation for you? I hope so.

WHAT'S YOUR COLOR?

The color of your urine can give you an indication of your hydration level. Naturally, the color of urine ranges from light yellow to almost clear. Its pigment becomes lighter the more

Water, Water, Water!

your urine is diluted with water. As weird as it sounds, you should regularly *see your pee*. Sorry, I couldn't resist. A better way to say that would be, regularly monitor the color of your urine to ensure you are not dehydrated. See how I cleaned that up? All jokes aside, let's talk about what the different pigments can mean. Again, light yellow to almost clear is the natural color of urine and considered to be healthy. But when too clear, it could mean you are drinking *too* much water and may need to cut back. Cloudy, orange, and dark brown, usually mean you are dehydrated. However, it can also be an indication of a diet change and medicinal side effects or more serious conditions like infections and diseases. If ever red or pink, it could mean blood is in your urine and is potentially serious.[19] See your doctor right away!

Most people never even notice or think about the color of their urine. The normal routine is to just release, wipe (if you're a female) and then flush (and please let's not forget how important it is to wash those hands). But knowing the color of your urine can give you clues on the condition of your health. You will then know whether to reduce your water intake, increase it, or if you need to go and get checked by your doctor. Stay alert! Make the decision today to see your pee!

ARE YOU HUNGRY OR THIRSTY?

It's a thin line between hunger and thirst. The same part of the brain is responsible for interpreting signals from both cravings; therefore, being dehydrated can cause you to think you need to eat something, when really, all you need to do is drink some good old H20. Similar symptoms of hunger and thirst are:

- Lack of concentration
- Dry mouth
- Sluggishness
- Lightheadedness
- Nausea
- Stomach pangs

Are you feeling any of the above symptoms? Your body is trying to tell you something. It is smart and knows how to send signals to indicate when it has a need. However, pinpointing these signals is not always easy. To differentiate between hunger and thirst, here are some things you can do:

- Eat every two to three hours and keep a record of your eating times.
- If you feel symptoms, drink some water first and wait ten to fifteen minutes to see if the symptoms subside.

Identifying your cravings will enable you to make the right choices for your body. You will know whether it's time to rehydrate or refuel. This will also help to prevent overeating which can lead to unhealthy weight gain. When your body starts talking, learn how to listen.

CHAPTER 6

STICK TO IT

I read a quote some time ago that is worth mentioning. It said, "You won't always be motivated, so you must learn to be disciplined" – Anonymous. If I was speaking this message instead of writing it, I would reiterate for emphasis. But I'll spare you the repetition and just tell you the message rings true. If I were to share the number of times I've wanted to give up while on this fitness journey, this book would have a lot more words and chapters. It would be the length of a novel. Some days, I felt defeated, as if I wasn't making any progress. Other days, my body didn't feel like making the sacrifice. And honestly, several days I wanted to eat like a pig. Some days, when I looked at someone else's progress compared to mine, I felt inferior (just keeping it real). Sometimes, I questioned if my goals were even obtainable. So no, you won't always be motivated, but if you're disciplined, and make the decision to be fit, you will stay the course and make progress.

CONSISTENCY IS KEY

Dictionary.com defines "consistency" as steadfast adherence to the same principles, course, or form.[20] In the words of best-selling author, philanthropist, and entrepreneur Tony Robbins: "It's not what we do once-in-a-while, that shapes our lives; it's what we do consistently."[21]

Not far from where I live, on a main thoroughfare, there's a man who parks his truck on a hill everyday with tomatoes loaded on the back. I didn't pay much attention the first few times I saw him, but one day, God spoke to my spirit and said, "Study the tomato man. Watch how he comes out here every day with his tomatoes." God talks to me like that. After a few months of watching, I noticed whether sunshine, or storming rain, he was parked in that same spot. Sometimes, I would pass by and see him; then hours later, on my way back home, he would still be right there with customers who had stopped to purchase his product. God spoke to me about him again and asked, "Do you see his consistency? There are many times when he sits for hours until customers come, but he stays right there until they show up. And because he's consistent, people take him seriously and he gets results."

Another example of consistency paying off is how my family embraced my fitness journey after watching my lifestyle change. Once I made the decision to do better, I went full speed ahead. At first, they thought it was a passing phase but after some time, they could see I was serious. During the Christmas season, we usually ask each other what we want as gifts, instead of guessing the wrong thing and ending up having a bunch of returns. But Christmas 2019, no one asked me anything and I thought nothing of it. But on Christmas day, as we all sat around opening gifts, every gift I received (from my husband, children, brother, and mom) was something related to fitness. I asked, "Did you guys discuss this?" The answer was, "No, we've just been watching you and knew what to do." And now some of them have joined this fitness walk with me.

I hope I didn't bore you with all those details, but my point is, no matter how difficult it gets, no matter how long you have to wait to see results, no matter who's on board with you and who is not, make the decision to be fit and stick to it. You will want to give up at times; your motivation won't always show up. But if you hang in there, eventually the results will follow. Take it from me and the tomato man: consistency pays off.

CHAPTER 7

THE KINGDOM PERSPECTIVE

My faith is the foundation of everything I do (you've probably picked that up by now). Therefore, I can never leave it out. In Chapter 4, I mentioned the Kingdom of God and will now explain it a little bit more. A kingdom is a territory ruled by a king. Within that territory, the culture is to carry out the will and the desires of that king. Often in biblical scripture, the phrases "Kingdom of Heaven" and "Kingdom of God" are used interchangeably, but there is a difference between them. The Kingdom of Heaven is an actual territory in an *unseen realm* where God's will is carried out by *spiritual* beings. The Kingdom of God is wherever God's will is being carried out on Earth by physical beings. How does this all relate to fitness? It is made clear in the following verse that being in good health and fit in every area of our lives are major desires of the King.

"Dear friend, I pray that you may enjoy good health and that all may go well with you, even as your soul is getting along well" (3 John 1:2).

Walking in good health is one way to honor the King through your body. In this healthy state, the Kingdom of God is present and operating through us. In what is called, "The Lord's Prayer," Jesus instructs His disciples to pray, "Thy kingdom come, thy will be done, on earth as it is in heaven." These words are powerful because saying them brings the influence of Heaven to Earth and commands God's will and purpose for our lives to come forth. When we speak these words, we are in many ways praying for the king in us to arise and execute God's will.

THE KING WANTS YOU

You are quite valuable to the Kingdom of God. Everyone was created and designed to be included in it. That creation comes with a purpose God wants to see fulfilled. Contrary to what many people believe, He wants His Kingdom to expand beyond the four walls of churches, beyond religious denominations, and circles to reach all areas of society. He wants people in every arena: media, arts, sports and entertainment, government, education, business and economy, science and technology, health and wellness, etc., to spread His influence and do what He created them to do.

What I want to bring out in all of this is, to whatever assignment you've been called, God wants you **FIT** for the journey. He desires healthy ambassadors to represent Him. I'm not discrediting, denying, or dismissing anyone, because like I said earlier, God can use whomever He chooses to get the job done. However, health and wellness are parts of Kingdom culture and attributes we should strive to display.

In 2 Corinthians 3:2, God's people are described as epistles (letters). This means our lives should be like letters, to those who have never read Scripture; or have read it but don't understand it; or have never entered a place of worship. They should be able to read our lives to see God's Kingdom in operation and desire it for themselves.

Being fit, in the full sense of the word, is to be in shape, suitable and well-equipped to meet a required response. Let that sink in. Take care of yourself. Take care of your body. Make fit decisions because the King wants you!

A FINAL WORD

You have now been given information that could change your life for the better; things you may not have known previously. There is now no excuse! You must bring responsibility on board and move into action. So, I ask, what are you going to do with the knowledge you've been given? Will you say, "okay, I've read the book" and then put it on the shelf? Or will you take responsibility for what you now know and do something about it? I hope the latter is your choice. If so, commit to the process by completing the accountability pledge on the following page.

May good health follow you all the days of your life.

ACCOUNTABILITY AGREEMENT

Congratulations! You've made it to the end of the book. That tells me you are serious about getting fit. I hope what you read has given you the knowledge and the faith to make a change in your lifestyle. Remember, faith without works is dead (James 2:20).

So, let's make your decision to work official. Please read the following commitment and then sign your name:

I want to live a healthier lifestyle. I choose to do the following three things from the book starting today:

1. _____
2. _____
3. _____

Accountability Agreement

I commit the next three months of my life to do the above activities fully and faithfully.

Sign: _____

Date: _____

After three months, pick at least one more thing from the book you can incorporate into your lifestyle and add it to the three above. Do this every three months for a year and before you know it, you'll be transformed.

Share your commitment with a trusted friend, spouse or partner that can hold you accountable. I'd love to hear about your progress. Please feel free to email me at fitdecisionz@gmail.com

Keep making fit decisions and you'll reap the rewards!

OTHER BOOKS BY SONNET FORD-GRANT

"What Should I Do?" A Practical Guide for Good Decision-Making.

"What Should I Do?" A Practical Guide for Good Decision-Making Companion Workbook

Available at: Amazon.com

NOTES

Notes

ENDNOTES

1. Ford-Grant, S. (2019). *What Should I Do? A Practical Guide for Good Decision-Making 2nd Edition.* Jonesboro: Sonnet Ford-Grant, LLC.
2. Forster, M. (Director). (2013). *World War Z* [Motion Picture].
3. *President's Council on Sports, Fitness & Nutrition (PCSFN).* (2018, February 27). From HHS.gov: https://www.hhs.gov/fitness
4. Dictionary.com. (2020, Retrieved May 2020). *consistency. 2020.* From Dictionary.com: www.dictionary.com
5. *Flexibility Exercise (Stretching).* (n.d.). From heart.org: https://www.heart.org/en/health-living/fitness/fitness-basics/flexibility-exercise-stretching#
6. Zwart, H. (Director). (2010). *The Karate Kid* [Motion Picture].
7. Centers for Disease Control and Prevention. (2012). Short Sleep Duration Among Workers. *MMWR Morb Mortal Weekly Report,* 281-285.
8. Institute of Medicine. (2006). Sleep Disorders and Sleep Deprivation: An Unmet Public Health Problem. *National Academies Press.*

Endnotes

9 John Hopkins Medicine. (n.d.). *Sleepless Nights? Try Stress Relief Techniques*. From hopkinsmedicine: www.hopkinsmedicine.org

10 Sleep Foundation. (n.d.). *Study: Physical Activity Impacts Overall Quality of Sleep*. From SleepFoundation.org: www.sleepfoundation.org

11 Diana Rodriguez (Reviewed by Aubrey Bailey, P. D. (2019). Lack of Physical Activity Can Contribute to Constipation (Bowel Movements Increase with Exercise). *Livestrong.com*.

12 Harvard Health Publishing - Harvard Medical School. (Updated: 2019, Updated: March 25). *Exercise is an all-natural treatment to fight depression*. From Health.harvard.edu: https://www.health.harvard.edu/mind-and-mood/exercise-is-an-all-natural-treatment-to-fight-depression

13 Hemsley, L. (n.d.). *5 Ways That Exercise Affects Your Sex Life*. From Aaptiv: https://aaptiv.com/magazine/exercise-affects-your-sex-life

14 Kotz, D. (2010, August 10). For Good Health, Watch Your Waist Size, Not Just Your Weight. *U.S. News & World Report*.

15 Robyn Webb, M. L. (2011, August). Eating Colorful Food Has Health Benefits. *The Healthy Living Magazine*.

16 Cleveland Clinic – Mental Health (2019). Don't Eat Until You're Full – Instead, Mind Your Hara Hachi

Bu Point. From ClevelandClinic.org: health.clevelandclinic.org

17   American Heart Association. (2018, April 17). *heart.org*. From Added Sugars: https://www.heart.org/en/healthy-living/healthy-eating/eat-smart/sugar/added-sugars#

18   Healthline Editorial Team. (2017, November 13). The Benefits of Vitamin D (Medically reviewed by Debra Rose Wilson, PhD, MSN, RN, IBCLC, AHN-BC, CHT). *Healthline.com*.

19   Watson, K. (2018, October 25). Is Blue Urine Normal? Urine Colors Explained (Medically reviewed by Gerhard Whitworth, RN). *Healthline.com*.

20   Dictionary.com. (2020, Retrieved June 2020). *consistency. 2020*. From Dictionary.com: www.dictionary.com

21   Robbins, T. (Retrieved May 10, 2020). *Tony Robbins Quotes (n.d.)*. From BrainyQuote.com: https://www.brainyquote.com/quotes/tony_robbins_147771

www.ingramcontent.com/pod-product-compliance
Lightning Source LLC
Chambersburg PA
CBHW071908070526
44583CB00016B/1903